Jeremiah Eames Rankin

Broken Cadences

Jeremiah Eames Rankin

Broken Cadences

ISBN/EAN: 9783337379605

Printed in Europe, USA, Canada, Australia, Japan

Cover: Foto ©Thomas Meinert / pixelio.de

More available books at **www.hansebooks.com**

BROKEN CADENCES

An Ode in Three Parts

BY

JEREMIAH EAMES RANKIN

BOSTON
OUR DAY PUBLISHING COMPANY
28 BEACON STREET
1889

TO JOSEPH COOK,

THE GREAT-HEART OF MANY

A PILGRIM

TO THE CELESTIAL CITY.

PART FIRST

THE CADENCES OF NATURE

BROKEN CADENCES.

PART FIRST: THE CADENCES OF NATURE.

I.

My childhood sense and vision
Of things elysian,
    How can I ever lose?
For all things that I see
Are more to me,
    If wet with life's fresh morning dews:
The light they keep, in which at first
They on my being burst.
    For, not a paltry thing of years,
    Whose sense grows dim and vision blears,
Can childhood be,
A transient ecstasy;
    It is God's kingdom, where
    He keeps all things unfolding fair;
Where every sight
Perennial yields a fresh delight;
    The colors cannot fade
    His hand upon them laid,

Have we the sense divine,
To know his touch and sign.

II.

The childhood spirit still shall find
The childhood mind.
If but life's burdens we unbind,
 Ourselves escape from brooding cares,
 If we but offer childhood's prayers,
The old time sights and sounds
Will burst their upland bounds,
 And flood our being unawares:
The stars eternal and the fragile flowers,
Regain their pristine powers;
 The sun will kindle hill and plain,
 And God in Nature smile again.
For, One once walked the paths of Palestine,
To whom the earth was all divine:
 The lily's white,
The sparrow's fall,
 The eagle's flight,
 The common day, and the transfigured night,
God was in all;
 No flower could bloom or leaf could stir,
But He could tell
Its meaning well;
 He was its best interpreter.
The film of sin is Nature's blight,
 Which shrouds her like a pall;
His touch that gave the blind their sight,
Can give us back lost childhood's light.

III.

That patriarch brow with crown of snow,
 Blanched white for Heaven,
  As though it caught the light
  From some celestial height;
As though celestial bloom

Irradiate from Heav'n's open room; —
   A child of seven,
A holier thing than it how can I ever know?
   And there it stands,
Eternal yet,
In those far morning-lands; —
My childhood faith can I forget?
That palsied pressure on my head
From wrinkled palm God's hand had led,
   Life's pilgrimage
   From youth to age,
It made my being consecrate,
It made my heart spring up elate.
   And still
   Go where I will,
I feel it there,
In blessing or in prayer;
   It thrills me through and through,
   And gives my life celestial impulse new.

IV.

The child that folds his dimpled palms,
   His mother's lap his altar, where
   He offers up his twilight prayer;
Still prattling, too, uninterrupted plays,
And mixing them with praise;
   Singing his vesper psalms,
   Till sleep his bark becalms,
And he is anchored fast
Within its placid bay at last;
   We dare not chide his lawless ways,
   Meanderings, and quaint delays;
And when he lies bedight,
In robes immaculately white,
We inward sigh, and wish that we
Could pattern take of his simplicity;
Could tread God's courts as he:
   We wish that we like him could sleep,

In a forgetfulness as deep.
When art would steal Heav'n's highest grace,
She paints a wingëd cherub's face;
   And God's own temple holiest,
   Is still the childhood breast;
And childhood's sleeping place
The spot the angels love to grace;
   While white before His burning throne,
   They never sleep,
   But their unbroken vigils keep,
   Lest little feet should trip against a stone.

v.

We all have inward yearning,
   A race heart-aching
   Never us forsaking;
   Unconscious sighing after God;
An instinct when represt
That brings us still the old unrest;
   A birthright through past lineage lost
   To be regained at any cost:
As when a pansy earthward trod,
   Its wounded stalk is turning
Up from the sod;
As though some organ grand should still retain
The echo of the strain
   Upon it played;
Should breathe it o'er again,
   As first essayed;
The disembodied spirit of melodious thought,
By some great master's hand into its being wrought;
   As though one in a foreign land,
   Should stoop with eager hand
To pluck a simple flower
That minded him of some long vanished hour;
   Vanished and fled,
   With mem'ry of his dead,
An instant back on its rare fragrance borne,

Then leaving him forlorn;
 As though one far from God and peace away,
 Should turn himself in sleep and pray;
 The inward man awaking in distress,
 And mutt'ring his half consciousness.

' VI.

All Nature has her litany.
One vast cathredral structure she,
Built without flaw or a defect
By the one great Architect.
Her mountains, columns of the blue, starred dome,
 Her caves peculiar shrines;
 Her pinnacles the murm'ring pines;
Her spire the cliff, the eagle's home.
The sons of God who kept the night, from their high
   beat retire;
Quenching in day, each torch reversed of fire.
 The morning breaks;
 Earth sends up incense from her hills and lakes.
From peak to peak all round the world,
As it from west to east is whirled,
 The high-priest sun goes lighting up her kindling
   pyres;
 Darting his leveled rays,
 Till all things are ablaze,
And every latitude aspires;
 And the round earth her homage pays
 To Him the Ancient One of Days.

VII.

I love to leave the world's rude throng,
To which I least belong,
And hear the thrush's song;
I love the water's liquid flow,
Which laughs and tumbles down below;
As though its art
Were frolicsome to part,

To keep us from a broken heart.
Like flocks of fresh-washed sheep,
The mountain torrents headlong leap;
    In vent'rous play,
    Shedding their tattered wool along the craggy
      way.
And, on old ocean's wrinkled shore,
The hooded monks prostrate implore;
Repeat their orisons forevermore.
    There is no voice which Nature uses,
    My listening soul refuses;
In tune I am with her,
A kindred and consenting worshiper;
    Her creed is mine,
    Her ritual and her every shrine;
For, He who made her, God, is everywhere
To hear the creature prayer,
    Which upward goes on incense-wings,
    From all insensate things;
And man can find Him there,
    And with Him walk, as Adam walked before,
    Through every consecrated corridor.

VIII.

To earth's kind countenance,
As to a mother's tender glance,
    I turn me when my heart is sad;
    One glimpse of her when I have had,
    Again my soul is glad;
    Me back has won,
    When lustreless the sun,
    And I had seemed heart-broken and undone.
The trees still clap their hands,
    The brooks are laughing loud,
And speeding through the meadow-lands,
    Their daisied banks they crowd:
    While on their brink,
    The giddy bobolink,

That has no time to stop and think,
Stoops down to drink, —
Nor tarries long;
Away he flies,
To greet the skies;
From water-beaded beak pours out his song:
Thus easing he his troubled breast,
In flight and song twice-blest;
Then, as if shot, drops to his nest;
Where his brown mate,
Mute with admiring love
For him above,
Presides in mother state.

IX.

Absence from God I cannot know,
Nor out of God can go;
The heart of Nature He,
To whom I orphaned flee,
And where He waits to bless
Me comfortless;
Her inmost shrine,
Where she finds out she is divine;
Reveals herself, as best she can
Unto God's alien creature man;
His temple, too, am I,
Swept and garnished from the sky.
I need no brooding sound,
Hov'ring a wingèd presence round,
To calm my spirit down,
To crown me with song's seraph-crown.
I climb earth's every altar-stair,
And find the God I seek, is there;
The rustling of his garments hear,
And kneel a worshiper;
See Nature's sights, breathe Nature's breath,
And through her learn what the Creator saith.
What mortal man has felt,

That still I feel;
Where mortal man has knelt,
    There still I kneel;
Earth has no fane, or shrine,
But has for me symbolic sign,
The cipher of the hand divine:
    Some outline caught
    From his eternal thought,
Some fair device in leaf or flower inwrought;
    The broken cadence dim,
.   The echo of that primal hymn,
Sung by the sons of God,
When first He arched the skies abroad;
    When first in that august processional,
    They answered his creative call; —
Creation's steps when first He lonely trod.

X.

Ye clouds that float in air,
    Above the farmer's labors,
Dappling the meadows soft and fair,
    Ye are my neighbors,
And ye bear
The semblance of my being there.
    For I, like you,
Am but God's breath,
    Floating across the blue,
From birth to death.
I've seen you white as Alpine snows;
To his repose,
    As by the angels in a long relay,
    I've seen the sun, by you like Nebo's prophet
        borne away,
    And then have turned aside to pray.
    Again, ye were to Heaven a Bethel way;
Some angel-trodden stair
Let down mid-way in air,
    Along the golden aisles of the departing day:

A dream surpassing sweet,
A wearied human soul to greet;
   Alone,
   Head pillowed on a stone.

XI.

Since dust I am and ashes,
Through which God's spark electric flashes,
   In all things made, I find,
   Myself am kindred to my kind.
I 've seen the autumn mountains clad in mist:
   I 've seen the sun arise,
And mantle them with amethyst,
And give the woods ten thousand dyes.
As though they marched in festal line,
To some far shrine,
   To pay creation's sacrifice;
Sealed with devotion's seal, signed with her sign.
The image they on Nature's page,
   Whatever transient thing he seize,
   His finite grasp to hold and please,
Of man's short pilgrimage,
   Between the two Eternities.
   A pageant just begun,
   When it is done.

XII.

I love to see each morn the sun,
   As though God said out of old night,
   Let there be light!
And it was done:
Creation's work renewed,
To waken daily gratitude;
   God's daily manual-sign,
   To show the work divine.
   I love to drink
Fresh draughts of morning air;
   To stand upon the brink

Of some bold precipice, and never shrink.
To see the new-born day come up
 Glad from the seas,
 Creep up the hills, and touch with skirts of light
  the dark fir-trees,
 And, conq'ring, every stronghold seize ;
Then heights of blue, meridian dare ;
To take each morn, as from an overflowing cup,
 In which God puts ingredients,
 To nourish new my every sense ;
 My very threefold being
 Transported with the seeing
Of things I cannot speak, my joy is so intense.
 The moon I love to see,
In robes of whiteness girt,
Peer through the woods which the horizon skirt,
 Walking alone in virgin purity.
 The skies, — time 's tent 'neath which the nations
  dwell ;
 The canopy, the Creator spreads
 Above man's clay-built sheds,
On which in rhythmic syllable,
He does his Godhead tell,
In phrase so simple that the child may spell ;
 In utt'rance so profound,
 That all Creation knows the sound, —
 The skies are nearer earth
 By day ; —
The sun retires, the sentry stars come out,
 And answer to the roll-call of their names,
 Crested with glory-flames ;
From the celestial host,
Along night's threatened front, each takes his post ; —
 Concave they lift themselves away ;
 The cords are straightened, and they rise ;
And holier thoughts in us have birth,
Aerial presences about.
The casement up, we look abroad,

And all things then are full of God.
The moon that climbs yon high ascent,
Now wimpled with a fleecy cloud,
    And then as though
    With her own toil aglow,
Her hood flung off, to tatters rent;
Is like some fair recluse,
From convent walls let loose,
    On greater solitude intent,
And heights serene allowed;
The scattered stars, devotion's sparks, that mark
Her pathway up the half-translucent dark;
    From unseen censer swung,
    The moving worlds among,
And left behind her on her sapphire way,
As nearer God she struggles up to pray.

XIII.

I love the country with its wholesome verities
    Of night and day;
    Its rising and its setting sun,
    Seen by God's creatures every one;
Its rude sincerities
    Of deed and tongue,
    God's unsophisticated folk among;
    Its kind asperities,
    Its soft austerities,
    Monitions true, moralities;
    And stern equalities;
Its work that's never done;
Its little time for play,
With scarce a respite or a holiday.
    I love the solitudes
    Of thick untrodden woods;
The sober stillness of stern winter's time,
Bearded, august, and reverend with his hoary rime,
    A patriarch creeping, doubled half,
    Upon his silver-headed staff;

Where'er I glance,
The trees snow-coated, as in moonlike trance.
I love the patient burdened brute;
All, tiny creatures mute;
The rabbit with his lifted paw,
Halting before he scampers off in awe,
I love the trackless snow,
  As though the God of Heaven
  The sinful earth had shriven;
Clothed her in his own spotless grace
To give her still a place,
  To walk again in white,
  Among the steadfast stars of night.
I love the winter's apotheosis when every twig is ice-
  encased,
And every bole with silver graced.
  And when the icicles
  Ring like ten thousand silver bells,
As though to some crusade;
To right the wrong of child or maid.
  I love the slow-returning spring,
  When budding life comes back to everything;
  To earth, and sea, and air,
  To Nature everywhere;
As though God took her by the hand,
  And whispered in her ear, Arise!
While miracles teem through the land,
  And bring us every day surprise.
In many a quiet vale,
The fettered brooks set free, resume their babbling
  tale;
  As though along their walk,
  Fresh learning how to talk;
Stern winter having made the elves
Soliloquize in undertone, or keep it to themselves.
  The birds
  Flock by in herds,
  Too full for sober words,

And pouring forth their notes
In liquid sparkles from full throats.
I love the summer, like a matron fair,
Binding fresh poppies in her golden hair;
The autumn dim, with its regrets
For every sun that earlier sets;
Its hazy atmosphere,
Its harvests undulating yellow,
Its fruits so luscious, pendent, trembling, mellow;
Its sibyl-leaves torn out, wind-wafted, sad and
sere.
Whatever Nature's costume or attire,
She still is my desire,
Of her I never tire;
She is my mother still,
Appareled how she will:
Fresh-cheeked or with her silver hair,
I have no thought or care;
I filial love her everywhere.

XIV.

There is a man of all the human race
Of whom, though loved the most, I cannot find a
trace;
With him I've stood beneath the throne immaculate
On which Mont Blanc holds his eternal state;
Gazed on his peerless altitude,
Till hushed was every purpose rude;
As ushered there before
The great Creator's temple door; —
With him, from childhood days my mate,
Have traversed rounded seas; —
But now he has outstripped my walk,
By such degrees,
I cannot with him as of old time talk;
His voice I cannot hear,
So full of manly and fraternal cheer;
And if I upward call, no answer back

Comes down from yon transcendent track;
What peaks he climbs I cannot know;
With verdure crowned or with eternal snow,
Or where to find him cannot go.
    And yet the sun
    Another annual journey has begun,
As though his manly form
Above the sod erect and warm
    Had still the old-time place:
    And from the skies
    Look down night's starry eyes,
As though his absence wrought them no surprise.
The year completes its round again,
As though it felt no pain;
    While all that I look on,
    To me speaks only of the one that 's gone;
    And earth at times seems but a room
    Contiguous to some lately open tomb.

xv.

With steadfast look beyond,
To continents unknown,
Whither we are drifting
'Neath winds that know no shifting,
    On tides that know
    No ebbing, as they mighty go;
To continents which there await
Our advent early or our advent late;
    What are earth's dreamings fond,
So quickly winged and flown?
Each bark we 've launched has faded out of sight,
    Like thread-rigged toys
    Put forth by little boys,
In their ephemeral delight;
    The product of the noise
    Which some half-holiday employs;
    Mimic frigates whittled out
    With many a loud, exultant shout;

No venture e'er returning,
With that consignment rich
Of silks and ores
In dreamed-of stores,
For which
Our poor fond souls were yearning.
   Wrecked they at sea, or on some distant shore,
   They come again no more;
So strong is our environment,
Our years so idly spent,
Our souls are so intent
On other things than what the Creator meant;
   So weak are we,
   And live we so uncertainly;
   We're like some struggler lost at sea,
   Who dissipates his energy
With crying out for help, instead
Of buffeting the waves, and bravely forging on
         ahead :
   We so forget our heavenly birth,
   And what to us God meant the earth.
While daily at her eastern gates,
The whole creation waits
   For that new man
   Who knows the Maker's plan,
Who in the creature the Creator knows;
Who finds Him in the rose,
That from his tropic culture queenly blows;
   Who finds Him in the Alpine bloom,
   That reddens full-veined next to Nature's tomb;
   Its every vital breath
   Defying the cold realms of death;
Who finds Him in the peak enthroned, twice-silvered
         by the moon
At night's high noon;
And in the plebeian weed,
Whirling triumphant on the chariot of its noxious
         seed;

And in the wayside violet,
Its lifted eye of trust with dew-drop wet
Who finds Him in the falling tear;
A rounded world of woe,
Which pearls all eyelids here blow;
Who finds Him in the circuit of the changeful year:
Four gospels manifold,
Bound with love's clasp of gold; —
To whom Creation is but Heaven's vestibule,
Where man himself may school
The living God to know,
As up to meet Him he shall daily go.
The God who once in Eden walked,
With dust and ashes talked;
The rustling of whose garments' fold
Was heard of old,
When murmured to the prophet's ear the mulberries;
In Shiloh's morning reveries,
When the prophetic vision lost through ways defiled,
God waked a little child;
Through him again began
To speak to man;
Was heard, when moaned the distant seas;
Deep calling out to brother deep
In that grand monotone,
Which every human heart has known
To be from God alone.
The distant seas which know no rest, and know no
sleep,
Time's pulses as for mortal tribes they keep;
The living God, who still supreme, alone,
Love's rainbow weaves around his throne;
But who has shown divinest grace
In One Man's death-transfigured face.

PART SECOND

THE CADENCES OF LIFE

BROKEN CADENCES.

AN ODE IN THREE PARTS.

PART SECOND: CADENCES OF LIFE.

I.

THE gentle one, unknown to fame,
Through whom my being came,
From whom I took the impulse of my human nature;
At God's creative word,
Which in earth's depths I heard,
Became a living creature;
Who bore me of herself a part,
Beneath the beating of her heart;
My pulse with hers as one,
Before I saw the sun;
When as a fabric fashioned at the loom,
Each tiny member found its room; —
Who tasted momentary death,
That I might breathe life's breath;
That I might feel life's glow,
Its gladness know:
Filial to her how back my thoughts will run!
For all things that are best,
By her pure soul imprest,

Came to be mine, through her at birth,
As water filters purer through the earth;
 Out of her chambered night,
 Comes bubbling up to light.
With an eternal mirth;
 That it at length has won
 These glimpses of the sun.

II.

 The tender hand,
 In that far childhood land,
That took my palms within her own,
 And folded them in prayer,
  To link me, morn and even,
  With God and Heaven;
That taught my feet to walk alone;
  The eager lips
  That kissed my baby finger-tips;
The voice from which I heard love's first sweet tone,
 From which in those far flow'ry days,
 I sucked the honey of first praise;
That taught me wond'ring there,
God was in earth and sea and air,
In all things grand, in all things fair;
 That lured my feet, so wont to stray,
 Into God's perfect way;
My mother's each; what tribute can I lay
Upon her dust, to-day?
  What tribute can I rev'rent wing
  To where she walks in white before the King?—
  I closed her eyes,
  That were my earliest skies;
In which I read celestial signs,
  From that first day,
  I caught their ray;
 To which I turned for rest,
 Amid the shadows of her west,
Though chiseled deep around, with sorrow's lines;

Composed her lips and face,
Which still had pensive grace ; —
Death durst not touch,
To mar her features much ;
Only to fix them there
More pure, more fair ; —
Imprinted kisses on the classic fullness of her brow
That almost chill me now ;
As though
'T were sculptured so,
The brow I 'd known,
And had the coldness of the stone ;
Took one last look,
Which all my manhood shook ;
And helped to bear her precious weight
Inanimate,
To its last resting-place.
How strict to Heav'n her thought !
How true to God she wrought !
So done her task divine,
As hews a workman to the line.
Her children were her earliest care,
Her children's children shared her latest prayer.
The pure in heart have one beatitude :
And in that sun she stood ;
For God she saw, and knew that He was good.

III.

Amid well-cultured lands,
I see the rounded hill-top, where the pars'n-
age stands,
Two sentry elms graceful before
The hospitable door ;
The apple-orchard planted near,
Where children come to swing,
And all their treasures bring ;
In spring, an outdoor room,
Fragrant with pink and snowy bloom,

What time the household robins sing;
And burdened low with fruit, on each alternate year.
Moss-marked, slow-yielding to decay,
I see the neighbor barns, that burst with garnered grain
    and hay.
Building their plastic walls,
With workman calls,   :
Which on my morning slumber fall
Intrusive all.
I hear the mason swallows 'neath the eaves.
I hear the wooden weather-vane, which all day grieves;
Wheeling incontinent about,
As though in doubt
What weather to turn out.
Rock-weighted at the end,
The long well-sweep I hear descend;
The bucket tumbling round,
With many a hollow and reverberating sound,
Till in cool depths is found
The water's bound;
      And bringing up its wealth,
      Cold-sparkling, full of life and health;
        While dripping backward musical,
        The overflowing contents fall.
I see adjacent fields, the well-knit farmers keep;
Guarding against the fowls, the seeds;
Battling the insects and the weeds;
I hear the constant murmur of the distant mills;
I see the circumjacent hills,
Besprinkled with the ever-moving sheep;
      The pink-eared lambs
      On timber-limbs,
    That haunt their anxious dams,
      And sore perplex them with their
        changing whims;
The great-limbed cattle, with their human eyes,
    That speak what speech denies,
    And have such large tranquillities.

Moving around, as though they knew God's plan,
In making them, and man.
   I hear the frugal bees,
   Speeding like rifle-bullets **where they please,**
   With undertoned soliloquies,
     And coming laden back
     Their instinct-guided track,
   With honey-buckets on their legs and knees.
I hear the stroke of partridge 'mid the trees,
The quail which shadows off by slow degrees,
     Till he to silence fade;
     Like some poor shade,
   Who haunts the earth till a neglected vow is
     paid,
   And then to peace is laid.

IV.

The meek-eyed maiden had an astral charm,
     The love-light hid,
     Beneath her drooping lid,
    Her autumn-colored richness shadowed by
     the flat
    Of her so graceful summer hat,
    Which seems forever lost,
When as a wife, she takes her husband's arm,
    Who sought her often purpose-crost;
   As though of high celestial birth,
She walked somewhere in Heaven, he plodding
    on the earth.
    The marriage service o'er,
    Along the lane, beneath the apple-bloom no
     more,
    Do they the lover's walk, arm-linked, ex-
     plore;
    Or murmur partings at the vine-clad door;
   Exchanging ling'ring kiss
   Beneath the clematis.
He owns her, as the land he owns,

In death, in life,
His hard-won wife,
And yet her as his queen enthrones;
And now content
With God's approval and consent,
Behind the plow, he plods again his farm;
The sidehill seeds to grain,
The sheep and cattle feeds again;
And with her, night and morning, kneels
To tell to God the gratitude he feels. —
In high monitions dim,
Which reach beyond thought's outer rim,
She far surpasses him;
In fibred fineness
And divineness;
By the great Creator meant
His complement;
Brought to the man
To finish out the perfect plan;
The capital
Of creatures all;
The crowning stone,
When the great work was done;
When God approving stood,
And saw and said all things were good;
Linking him on Heaven's side,
To Christ, the Crucified,
In love's eternal plan,
Of woman born, and not of man:
In Eden once his bane, his loss,
His gain eternal by the Cross;
Now walking loyal at his side,
His better conscience and his guide. —
Beyond the heights which scarcely he can spy,
She angel-winged, can fly;
Can inward listen to the seas
Which break from the eternities;
Can hear their solemn moan

When most she is alone.
And yet all day she sits and sews,
Or knits him woolen hose,
As he takes animal repose,
Content that while he sleeps, all Nature grows;
She golden butter makes,
And browns to suit his eye the wheaten cakes,
Or studies how to mitigate his woes and aches.
He calculates his crops of grass and corn,
And for the city
Feels self-complacent, philosophic pity,
And a kind of unarticulated scorn.
For what to him were city-life, but life in jail,
Without the need of giving bonds, or getting bail?
However interpreted or turned about,
Man shut in to man, and God in Nature, all shut out?

v.

I would not underrate
The task severe,
When woman girds herself, to save the
home or state,
And not because she thinks it grand or
great,
To fill some outward sphere!
Who hears some thunder-tone
As though from God alone,
Some whisper in her loneliness,
To stem the tide of earth's distress,
And leaves the cradle, for the battle or the throne;
Making a martyrdom
Of her own heart and home.
Where her heart bleeds,
There must she stand for human needs.
But ah, the woman's breast,
Which never has been prest
By tiny thumb of babe in sweet unrest,
Lips trembling like the petals of the rose,

In his repose,
As back and forth the tide of being flows!
She who, as mother, ne'er looks down
Upon the shad'wy baby crown,
The earthly years are weaving for his brow,
Knows not what thing it is to be entirely
blest;
Whatever guerdon rare, she may win now.
For next the heart of God,
Who in the flesh earth's pathways trod,
'T is woman's part
To bear man's burdens on her heart;
And human motherhood
Must ever brood
O'er all earth's ills the compensating good.

VI.

The mother with her children round her knees,
Is always at her ease.
Their curious questions she can answer them;
Explain their quaint unfoldings
Of things in first beholdings;
Can multiply their blisses
With repetitious kisses;
Interpret all their guesses,
Bring balm to their distresses,
Nor leave the garment's hem,
She stitches with industrious degrees.
Upon the cradled babe she keeps her eyes,
The latest advent from the skies,
And murmurs low her lullabies;
Weaving a hammock round
Of soothing sound,
In which she sacred lays him;
Then back and forward sways him.
A kind of finite providence,
Which like the dew among the flow'rs distills;
Having of childhood ills

The constant sense;
Its woe wise to console, its wants she complements.

VII.

The wealth of molten gold,
Coiled up in woman's hair,
The sunlight there,
When it is braided fold on fold,
And crowns her like a coronet;
What is an ornament more fair?
Disloyal man, do not forget,
Home is her own peculiar realm;
Own her home's queen, and swear allegiance.
For, no Greek goddess she in mail and
helm;
Thine equal made,
To love thee, and not be afraid;
Taken thy counterpart
From near thy heart.
Downcast and modest is her glance,
An open book her countenance;
Two deep-blue pansies are her eyes,
Which have the kindness of the skies.
To have from God a part
In such a woman's heart,
To call her all his own,
Flesh of his flesh, bone of his bone,
Joint-heir with him to a celestial throne,
Is sweetest of man's finite destinies.

VIII.

Home's simple worship round our altar said,
Love's parting rites are paid,
And vanished is the little cavalcade.
Encamped they lie on slumber's hills,
Amid the lulling rills,
Beneath green trees,
That ripple in the breeze. —

We part to sleep, as though we sought new hemi-
    spheres;
Were sundered by relentless years;
As though we crossed wide seas,
Which bear us where they please,
    Long leagues afar
    From 'neath home's star;
In sleep may pass death's gate,
And then remorses are too late.
    We stand, the quick with 'bated breath,
And through its iron grate,
        Look on our loved ones in the lunar light
            of death;
Are still,
And know God's will.
        To old conditions, vain
        Our struggle to adjust ourselves again;
Earth cannot over make
Herself, for those, whose life is but heart-ache.

IX.

The open grate is like a cynosure
Me from myself to lure;
    And crackling embers have for me
    A magic ministry;
        So thickly fraught
        Are they with all creative thought.
Musing alone,
Day's labors done,
    Here all horizons blend,
    As at life's end.
        The hour
        Has mystic power
To give me back my own:
    My old-world sires,
        Who westward came to kindle freedom's fires,
Amid the sombre silences
Of forest trees;

To build their humble rough-hewn walls
By lonely waterfalls,
Where distant mountains frown,
Or show the rosy glory of their winter's crown. —
Tracing thought's chain, thus link by link,
Myself I backward think,
To those state-builders there,
Who wielded well the axe, and knew the
power of prayer. —
And, then, surpassing fair,
All diademed with light,
As though plucked from the brow of night
Comes back the babe from earth translated,
Before a year was dated;
Comes back the man-strung, ardent youth,
With eye aglow with fire and truth,
And life's fair promise heavy-freighted;
The chords he touched, unstrung,
His rhythmic thoughts unsung,
His name unknown
Save to home-hearts alone:
As well as he,
Who loved me passing well
Beyond what tongue could tell,
Who should have lived to mourn for me.

X.

I love to think of childhood days,
When all things wrought in me amaze,
And when I went,
As though to other life some incident,
Through years all June,
Humming an untaught tune,
Like bee led on by subtle scent,
And with life's affluence all content;
Floating an idle circumstance,
As bubbles on a streamlet dance;
Encounter whatsoever chance.

I love to think of childhood sports, and childhood
    schools;
Of wading knee-deep in the lilied pools,
Although it fractured all the rules;
    Of comrade boys,
    So full of stratagem and noise,
    So bent upon illegal joys,
    They often lost their equipoise;
Of golden-headed girls,
Half-buried in their wealth of curls;
    So fresh and neat,
    Like half-unfolded blossoms sweet,
Accoutred in their muslin dresses,
Their cheeks still flushed with home-caresses;
    And eyes that spoke their meaning,
    In spite of their long lashes' screening.

XI.

    The urchin with his barbëd hook,
    Who loves the shadows of the alder-brook,
For minnows angles or the glancing trout,
His bait reluctant wriggling in and out:
Some wretched earth-worm dug
From out the turf with many a tug;
    Is shy of work, and shy of book.
And when his sluggish thought expands,
He dreams of winds that waft to other lands,
    Of tropic islands far,
    Where heights volcanic are;
Where 'neath the fronds of tow'ring palm,
Break with their lulling spray, great seas of calm;
    Where tropic fruit perennial grows,
    And languid air wooes to repose.
His future lot, —
His humbler native haunts forgot,
    His pulse abated to a manlier rate, —
To heed his country's call
And guide the course of some tall admiral,

Piled to the very sky with sail,
Majestic moving on before the gale,
    Till she shall into foreign harbor ride,
    And long disputed rights decide;
Great themes to arbitrate;
To settle questions large of state,
Big with a nation's future, or her fate.

XII.

    They say,
    The owls and owlets gray,
    " Alack, alack a day,
    The earth, decrepit, soon will pass away."
    But all the babes that dance and spring,
    Do not believe the thing;
Nor do their mothers in whose eyes
Are kindled such high prophecies.
    And all the boys beneath the sun,
    Who think things made for fun,
        Who every stray pedestrian greet
        With laughter on the street,
    Believe that time is just begun.
    They have their manners droll,
        Their mystic dialect,
        Their projects from their elders to protect;
    Their hoops they roll,
        Their marbles play,
        And round each season's course away,
        As though life were some holiday.
And every little shapely maid,
In pink and white arrayed,
    Who watches glad their sport,
    Has notions of the self-same sort.
For every generation still renews the earth,
As though it had from God's own voice its birth. —
    To them the old man on his staff,
        Beneath the burden of his years,
    Low bending up in half,

And not the earth appears,
Worn out;
And so with song and shout
They greet her not with tears.

XIII.

I love a little child to meet,
Meandering through the maple-shaded street,
To feel his tiny hand creep in my own;
The fingers there divine
Clinging to mine,
As round the trellis close the tendrils of the vine;
To hear his confidential undertone,
As though 't were all for me alone,
No king upon his throne,
Has sceptre wide as he;
No wise man in his academic seat
Can him of bliss defeat,
Or with the wisdom of his talk compete.
Straight to the mark his intuition goes,
Hitting his friends as well as foes,
Though oft his craft he little knows.
He questions asks like Socrates,
Of whom, of what it him may please;
Interrogates
Of deeds and dates,
And scarce the answer waits.
In every flower he takes delight,
Puts every quadruped to flight,
His tortuous way pursuing after
With large, abundant laughter.
Hat off, he makes some dash,
As quick as lightning-flash,
And as you turn,
His last intent to learn,
Holds up before your eyes,
The rarest of all butterflies.
While gold-dust lingers

Upon his fingers.
His eyes are everywhere,
With their inquisitorial stare;
Of every thing he is aware;
Alert to challenge it,
The heart of it to hit,
With the unfailing shaft of his untutored wit.

XIV.

I love to kiss a boy,
With great heart in his little breast,
And pulse which knows no rest,
Who finds supremest joy
In every sport and toy;
Whose liquid eyes
Take color from the skies.
With just enough of earth
To justify his human birth;
Augustan, shapely face,
And germs prophetic of all manly grace;
That scarcely feels the ground,
Elastic so his bound;
As though his feet
Were winged, his destiny to meet,
Angelic-arched his brow,
A temple where high thoughts brood now;
Strange boyhood aspirations,
Hov'ring to fix their habitations;
As doves light on a roof, they do not know,
Then rise in flight to go,
With single motion on their wings of snow;
As mist around the mountain altitudes,
In early morning broods,
As though to stay;
Then floats away,
Rose-tinted on the breath of breaking day. —
Half-cherub he,
The other half our poor mortality;

And only God can know,
Whether his future years shall grow
To blessing or to woe.
Above the hum
Of school-house scenes,
He hears the twirring of the troubled drum,
As though it knew the woes to come,
This boy not in his teens;
His spirit answers quick,
Keeps time within,
To its strong movement and its din,
And swarming fancies gather thick;
Within his bosom rise,
As from the skies,
Awakened prophecies.
The stirring bugle sounds,
His heart would burst its bounds;
He hears within some trumpet-call,
Though what it means, he does not know at all.
The soldier he, in germ,
Waiting his manhood's term,
Till muscled for the battle-shock;
The martyr, dauntless he before the block;
The poet, prophet, priest of some half-blossomed day,
When better thoughts men's lives shall sway,
Nor will they be ashamed to speak of God and pray.

XV.

The humble college-halls which stand
Embosomed in a mountain land;
Whose windows, east and west,
See what is grand in Nature, what is best:
Beneath, on every hand,
The strong-soiled intervales expand,
Under the stalwart farmer's hand; —
From yonder height, the lake which flashes blue;
With white-winged bark
Gliding its waters dark,

The landscape op'ning ever new
To the enraptured view;
The reptile river, creeping treach'rous 'neath the alder-
trees,
Now flashing in the sun, then hiding as from sight it flees;
Where we were wont young limbs to lave,
The daring leap, or headlong plunge to brave,
Or with the feathered oar,
To steal along the shadowed shore; —
The crested steeps which tempt feet upward to explore;
To win at length
A nobler poise and strength;
To which we turn, for counsels wise,
When, wearied brain and eyes,
The thought of books we half despise;
How gratefully we think of these,
Whene'er we backward gaze
In manhood's after days.
O modest mother of a noble race,
Content to be unknown,
If but the seed thy sons have sown
May wave in golden grace!
Can we forget the kindly matron face,
Which gave our boyhood timid, rude, a welcome there?
Can we forget the Christian care,
Of those who filled each humble place?
Ephem'ral honors come to men
Through sword and pen;
A line we write
As if in golden light;
A deed attain,
Which cannot be undone again;
We gain a laurel-leaf,
A wheat-head for our harvest-sheaf;
God took their lives and set them where
They shine eternally and fair;
Rev'rent to man and God, loyal and true,
The praise we give to them is more than due.

XVI.

I would not wear the nimbus of a saint;
Owe it to canvas and to paint;
 However slight the part
 Of limner's art;
Be rather that eschewed
For the beatitude
 Of being simply brave and good;
 A man to whom a child,
 Ingenuous, undefiled,
 Might run with pleasure wild,
 To be of petty grief beguiled;
  Of whom a soul to sin betrayed:
  Or reckless lad, or hapless maid,
  To tell their fault would never be **afraid.**
I would not walk the tangled maze
Of one who truth withholds, or truth betrays;
Elects the serpent's crooked ways: —
Nor will I drink his siren cup of praise.
  Nor do I care
  Again to join with him in prayer.
 His God and mine
 Are not alike divine.
 With him I break,
 Another path to take;
 Walk where are thorns,
 Although my comrade scorns;
And walk invulnerable,
  For every word of human blame
  Shall be at length a tongue of flame,
My real deed to tell,
 And give it fame.

XVII.

 Faith's nutriment I find,
Not in God's Written Word alone,
But in the moss-grown stone,

The ground-bird hides her nest behind;
And in the spotted oval forms
Her little body warms,
Until they spring
To life on wing:
Her fledglings, that shall soar and sing;
In every tiny brook that turns
The schoolboy's water-wheel;
In every flower that yellow burns
Beneath the plowboy's heel;
In all of life from God; for He is there,
As well as in the solemn cadences of hymn and prayer.
And so I live on earth to learn of Him and
Him to love,
Till He shall call me to another school
above.

XVIII.

From age's craggy heights of snow,
Through clouds that drifting go,
I catch a glimpse of what is still below:
Green intervales with floating shadows;
And herds that sprinkle shapely meadows;
Elms graceful, and so queenly,
Swaying their robes serenely;
The harvest-fields of gold,
That yield their hundred fold;
The haunts familiar, where the children play
The livelong day.
I hear, or seem to hear,
Their laughter wafted upward on the breeze,
To greet my dulling ear,
As through the lonely snow-capped trees,
I from earth's visions disappear;
More lost to view, each passing fear,
Soon gone from sight and sound,
On heights still more profound;

Those peaks no mortal soul has trod,
Which lift themselves, till they are lost in God.

XIX.

No mortal takes his being's altitude;
Beneath his Maker's sight
　　Grows to his height,
　　As grow the cedars high
　　Against the sky,
Projected lone
On snow-crowned Lebanon;
However swell his heart elate,
Whate'er ambitious Babel call him great,
How high he stands in church or state;
　　Whate'er his earthly road;
Until by Calvary he 's stood,
Until faith's stars above him brood,
　　And he has domed his life in God.
Only the great Master's hand
Can the soul's full harmony command;
　　Has skill to smite
　　Its chords aright;
Can hush its strings to trembling silence quite;
　　Or from it bring
　　Life's grand orchestral offering.

XX.

Ah, what cares Nature when we cease to
　　breathe?
Through all her constant hours, ˉ
Out of our dust, she thrifty makes her flowers;
　　Her em'rald carpet weaves,
　　Dappled with overhanging leaves;
Nor cares although no hand our marbled brows
　　shall wreathe.
　　　Words few are said;
　　　The knitting turf above our head,
Beneath the healing rain,

Grows green again;
She feels no pain,
But on her pathway wheels amain,
In spite of death's fresh scars,
Among the stars.
Morning and night, the mountains purple still;
The maples dome the once familiar hill;
The glad brooks run
Beneath the sun,
And the same valleys fill
With babblings, like a child who utters all his will.
But if our life is hid with Christ in God,
The humblest sod
Which we have trod,
Our feet with preparation shod,
Becomes a shrine
Almost divine;
Our life still onward flows,
As when the sun has set, gleam afterglows,
That have the color of the rose;
And kindling stars take up the light,
To glorify the night.

THE CADENCES OF ART

BROKEN CADENCES.

AN ODE IN THREE PARTS.

PART THIRD: THE CADENCES OF ART.

I.

I SEE Art's archetypal forms
In the prolific norms,
With which all Nature swarms.
The fir projected heav'nward higher
Becomes the Gothic spire;
Whose tip the setting sun lights up with fire:
   The ragged cliff, where eagles hover,
    Sailing upon strong-pinioned wing,
  With unsheathed eye their prey discover,
    Its path high-shadowing
    Ready precipitated to alight
    On it with lightning flight,
Becomes the citadel
    Round which an outraged people swell,
     Their threats and bruit
     Dashed at its foot; —
      As when a sullen sea
      Retires resentfully,
    Swallowing its wrath
    Along its backward path; —

The baron there
His pennon on the air,
Gnashing his teeth, like wild beast in his lair.

I.

To cap the column,
That fronts some temple solemn,
I see the marble from the quarry's womb
To lily whiteness bloom;
Beneath the master's stroke
Become the classic laurel or the oak;
As alabaster pure
The wrought entablature;
The stone unfold the while
In lotus blossoms from the Nile;
In Nature's various leaves and fruits,
In scrolls and fronds and convolutes;
Acanthi curling in and out
The capitals about;
The clusters of the vine,
—Which purple mantle, with their fragrant wine,
Full-hanging as for golden chalice,
In hall or palace,
Where guests shall rise
To pledge the light in beauty's eyes,—
Festooned in many a place
With native negligence and grace,
And clinging to the stone,
As though they thus had grown:
The product of some arctic mould,
Where Nature works her wonders manifold;
Makes crystal flowers
Through all the winter hours;
The spectral dual of the spring,
When life full-veined, comes back to everything.

III.

For Nature is but the Creator's School of Art,
Where He suggests the part

Left for the finite hand to do;
Out of materials crude
Around profusely strewed,
After his models careless thrown,
By which He would be known,
To beautify the earth and make it new.
As children who should play, they wrought
In clay or stone
In answer to their father's thought.
And God has domed the earth with blue,
The arch with crystals fraught,
Made forests grave,
Outstretched their leafy architrave,
And groined their intertwining branches
brave;
Has pearled the grass with dew,
And all for study brought.
As He should say:
" Thus dome your temples of a day;
Your necklace string,
From pearls that divers bring,
From diamonds of the mine,
That in the sunlight flash and shine."

IV.

The twin cathedral steeples of Cologne,
—That temple of white stone,
Which casts its spectral shadows in the Rhine —
Like two tall trees arise,
Slow growing through the centuries,
As when a pine from some prolific cone,
Is left on mountain heights to tower alone; —
Symmetrical in every line,
Shad'wy, dim, and half-divine;
Complete at length,
And graceful in their strength,
And undulating to the eye,
As trees when light winds pass them by:

As fragile as the fabric of a dream,
Or image in a stream,
  Yet of the wheeling earth a part —
As though by the Creator meant,
Original, constituent,
 And held by magnet to her central heart.

v.

  Great Guido gets his hints
   Of morning tints;
   Of floating forms,
   Which vital color warms;
  Move on the air
  As though to it they native were,
From clouds that drift him by:
God's artist-palette, set up in the Italian sky.
  In the Apollo Belvidere,
  Angelic, beautiful, severe,
  The sculptor could but mould
  After God's model old,
What first He did in his great masterpiece:
  The man original,
  Ere his disastrous fall.
The arrow given release,
  The postured huntsman stands
With muscled frame,
And pulse the stone's chill cannot tame;
  The bow still in his hands,
With sinews strung,
Eternal, strong, and young.
  On wing the arrow flies
  And there the victim lies
  In his last agonies.—
   The sculptor knocks
   At portals of the rocks;
 The echoes wake,
As though imprisoned there,
Transcendent, fair,

Were some rare form, whose heart would break,
    Unless allayed her long despair;
    Unless she breathed this mortal air;
Some captive creature of the seas,
Entombed there through the centuries.
    He inward toils to liberate
    This white ideal from her fate;
      Until his hidden thought
      Is to expression's body wrought:
      Her very life and being caught;
The grace which crowns his perfect art,
Has pulsing life, and beating heart;
    And delicate and dainty stands,
    A dream in stone set free by mortal hands;
      Disrobed to day;
      Her cold environment cut clean away.

VI.

I walked a city's rounds alone, —
A hamlet to a city grown, —
    Where I had once in boyhood played.
The tiny brook revisited,
Where many an hour in sport had sped;
The pool where I was wont to wade,
Where I had headlong dared the shelving brim,
And learned the art to swim.
    I could not find a spot
    To answer to my early thought;
      Proportions all were lost,
      My every recollection crossed;
    Leaning awhile,
    Against the moss-grown stile,
      Which oft in glee I'd climbed,
      When childhood-limbed,
    With eyelids dim,
    I back to mem'ry brought
Many a lad and little maid,
Who tripped with me the everglade,

As once we sought
The Mayflower and forget-me-not.
Though still the same
Earth's outward look,
To outward eye
The hill, the sky,
The purling brook,
The sweet briar's breath;
I catalogued name after name,
That had been starred by death. —
I stood at length, beneath the statue in the park,
And there my first companion came to mark:
The man who shook the Senate in debate,
Who saved the State!
The rest were dead and gone,
The man in bronze lived on.
His form had walked through furnace-flame
To be eternally the same.
To me
More real he,
Than all the dead, than all the living small
great.

VII.

Sam Adams standing there
Upon yon Boston square,
Is speaking still
Across to Bunker's Hill,
His arms firm-braided with defiant will.
What the great Webster thund'rous said,
Was greater than the granite shaft above
his head;
And what the Continental fathers wrought,
Behind the fife and drum,
Was greater than the sum
Of the great Webster's greatest thought.
Upon that sacrificial mount,
The cost to them they did not count;

Death's cup for man they quaffed;
  And so the constant sun
    That lately left the crumbling pyramid,
    And all the mystery of death it hid,
    That lately left the sphynx, half-buried in
      the sand
  Of that night-shadowed land,
  Irradiates yon shaft
  When first he leaves the sea,
And when the day is done,
And he sinks down to rest,
In seas beyond the Great Republic's mighty
    west,
  With bloom of immortality.
At Gettysburg, what Lincoln said,
  The martyr's aureole about his head,
    Bivouacked around,
    That cloud of witnesses in consecrated
      ground,
      He spoke,
      Because
      Of what he was;
    A lightning rift was made
    That rent the battle's shade,
    And open vision came again
    From God to men.
  And still we give our thoughts a pause,
. At every periodic clause,
    As though we heard
    Some high prophetic word,
A message from the Lord,
Struck from a Hebrew prophet's chord:
  The seer's silence then he broke.
  He saw the final issues there
  Had come in answer to the bondsman's prayer;
    Were but the riper fruit
    Of Freedom's uncorrupted root;
That smitten was that sea of blood,

To let God's Israel through dry-shod.
His providential part
Beyond the power of oratoric art;
Beyond the gift and grace of schools,
Beyond all rigid rules;
An inspiration given,
As though anointed he of Heaven.

VIII.

The orator I see, poised like a figure grand,
That's cast in bronze, Time's changes to withstand,
An instant caught at rest,
On thought's high crest,
Erect as on the ear his cadence calls,
Like echoes far of waterfalls,
That men may wake,
And list'ning take
Dimension of his larger thought
And to the level of his flight be brought.
Around the soul the spell
He weaves what words can tell?
An oracle,
In whom the secrets of the future dwell;
Eternity's ambassador
Whose accents knock at the soul's door,
And haunt her corridors forevermore.
He speaks; each phrase by coming phrase
outdone,
Until thought's steep is won.
As when some tree that winter has encased,
Its limbs with silver armor graced,
The whole by crystal coat entwined,
Uplifted by the wind
Which all its twigs and branches twirls,
Besprinkles pearls:
The ear entranced before
Still craving more.
So speaks the Greek Demosthenes;

Against the Macedonian plies his pleas:
And so the Christian heralds come
From Paul, through shining ranks of martyrdom,
To many a modern Chrysostom.

IX.

I love the poet's verse,
Whose measured cadences break like incoming
seas;
Stir me within, the while my outward sense they
please;
Whose trumpet-tones rehearse
Man's deeds divine,
In ev'ry pulsing line.
Whose word within an echo wakes,
As when along cathedral-aisles the organ breaks;
And nerves the soul, inspired to dare
The deed it asks of God in prayer.
In rapt Isaiah's verse I see,
The God-Man in humility;
The matchless Form appears,
The First Born of earth's coming years.
To Shakespeare with expansive brow,
The temple of his fine intelligence,
The throne
Where he sits king alone,
The princely sceptred mind
Of all the human kind,
With all the world I bow,
With gratitude intense;
As though to me were opened some
new sense.
To Goethe bow, self-poised, self-centred and sus-
tained,
Like Jupiter on the Olympian height he's gained,
And sunning his colossal nature there,
Luxurious in thought's upper air.
And bow to Coleridge, with his dreamy solitudes,

And tideful moods
          Of mystic utterance;
          A Delphic seer in rhapsodic trance.
And Wordsworth on his meditative task serene,
With philosophic pause and mien,
          And introspective eye,
          I love to walk near by;
     Hear him discourse of boy and man, of earth
          and sky,
     And echoes catch from thought's eternity.
          I love, too, lyric Robert Burns,
          To whom all Nature turns,
          With startled, virgin look
          To be set down within his book.
And limping Byron, seamed and scathed,
On climb volcanic, lava-pathed,
          With pilgrim wallet, and with staff,
          The Alps still echoing to his cynic laugh;
          Like some archangel, clipt of wing,
          But still intent to mount and sing.
     And Robert Browning, with his cumbered line,
          Big with enigma, and involved design,
Bigger with brain;
An eagle's flight along thought's higher plain;
          While men gaze up to see him there,
          Inhaling what to him is air,
          And panting in their half-despair.
               And his Elizabeth,
          His queen,
          Coequal throned by double right serene;
               Twin star with him, holding her way
               Along the paths of day;
               Breathing alike the poet's breath,
          And rising from her grief's eclipse
          To taste love's honey from his lips,
               And to defy the worst of death;
Her curl-encompassed head
          In Florence laid;
          Beneath the sky

Of her adopted Italy,
Where many a pilgrimage is made : —
He lies with England's greatest dead.
    And Alfred Tennyson,
    Man's titled lord, God's titled man in one.
        And Bryant, breathing woodland breath,
        With his immortal look on death.
And brown-thrush Whittier, with his Quaker coat,
And Holmes, the mocking-bird, with various note,
        And him, New England's truest son,
            Primeval mass unbroke,
            That never felt the hammer's stroke,
            Rose-tinted quartz in block,
            Thrown up by Puritanic shock,
        Ralph Waldo Emerson.
And him with song so ripe and mellow,
        The polished poet-priest,
        Whose barque comes always golden-fleeced,
Our German-English, sweet Longfellow.
        And e'en Walt Whitman, too,
        Wayward and rude
        Among the poets' gentler brotherhood,
        Whose backwoods' tramp befits America the
            new ;
    The stalwart poet on his western way
            To where Pacific's gate
            With ready fold
            On hinge of gold
        Does for the future wait,
Flashing in light of dying day.

X.

I love to rise from sleep
        And seek creation's Lord a room,
          In which to keep
The daily passover, before to toil I go ;
To meet a fate I do not know.
Ere yet the morning-red has made the mountains
    bloom,

I love the notes
Of music on the morning air,
Amid unbroken stillness there;
Before earth's denizens awake,
And up their daily burdens take;
Before the morning's hurried dash,
The din of traffic and machinery's crash,
While yet the shadows cool
Fall on the trembling pool,
Ere yet a single nook is stirred
By twitter of a bird,
Or strident insect chord is twirred.
I love the sound of cornet, viol, flute,
When all things else are mute.
Up from the valley far it floats
As floats a prayer. —
Without or fragrant pine, or gnarlëd oak,
Without the shock
Of blasted rock,
Without the hammer's stroke,
As shapely architecture to the skies,
So have I heard a temple fair arise
Of close-compacted harmonies;
Its ground
The depths of sound
Profound;
The echoing vaults,
Where human cadence halts:
Its heights
Pinnacled with angel flights,
And floating far,
As to some list'ning star.
These are the structures high, that roll
Their empire o'er the captive soul,
Built by the great tone-architects,
As man from stone, cathedrals grand erects;
Rising in their eternal cadences
As rise the earth around

In hymns of high degrees,
The wakened seas.
    So Handel and so Haydn wrought
    Within the secret mines of thought;
    Beethoven so, and Mendelssohn
    Built great tone-fabrics to the sun.

XI.

Where Titian once has laid his brush,
    My very breath I hush;
Where Rubens' canvas florid blows,
With tint of flesh or tint of rose,
    I warm with spirit flush.
    I rev'rent stand below
    The work of Michael Angelo;
Who Hebrew Moses wrought,
The stone responsive to creative thought;
    Who sprang St. Peter's dome,
    Another sky beneath the blue of Rome.
Alike on life-hued canvas, or in death-hued
    stone,
I find not mortal man alone;
I find the Hand which guides the hand,
Which answers Art's demand,
    As older hands are wont to guide
    The tiny palms which awkward slide
        And mar the page
        Of childhood's pilgrimage:
To Phidias and Thorwaldsen given,
The one same gift of Heaven.

XII.

To think of woman as a flower
To pluck from parent stem;
    Made for the pastime of an hour,
     And not thy life with love to dower;
     To clothe thee with diviner power,
    And hand in hand

With thee to stand
Upon the borders of the Morning Land;
To think of woman as a star
To wile from her high sphere afar,
    Thy hand to gem,
    Thy head to diadem,
    A slave to kiss thy garment's hem;
And not thy goodlier counterpart,
With God to share thy heart,
Thy power to beautify the earth with truest art;
  Is to deny life's best beatitude.
    For man alone is never man;
    'T is fracture of God's plan,
    Not so the primal purpose ran:
      Else Eden's solitude
      Had been the greater good.
    As his is true her note of song,
    Her artist touch as light, its stroke as
      strong;
    Her speech
    Thought's rudiments can teach;
    Alike thought's higher realm can reach.

XIII.

    The widow clad in solemn serge,
    Of weeping always on the verge,
      As though to nurse her grief
      Were her relief,
    Her lids oft wet
    To think some time she may forget;
A babe within her arms
Made up of dimpled charms,
  And innocent alarms,
Across whose face the lights and shadows play
As on an April day;
    Plucking his mother by the ear,
And playing with the pictures in her eyes,
And feigning his fictitious ecstasies;

Her red-ripe lips
With tiny finger-tips
 Aside disposing,
 Her teeth of snow disclosing,
And asking questions which she does not
  hear;
Her glance oft far-away,
As though some destiny forbade on earth her stay;
 As though her soul were stirred
 By some strange voice she heard;
  As though there were some beckoning hand
   unseen,
  That still would intervene.
Reluctantly she lives. But ere she dies,
This babe that now his cunning plies,
To wile the sorrow from her eyes,
Has grown to fame the power of death defies:
 Her face delineated as a saint,
 Madonna or a Magdalen,
 That draws the gaze of men;
Or framed her grief to song,
Such as the ages will prolong;
 Or draped her matron form to stand,
 Symbolic at the gateway of some noble land
  With Freedom's torch uplifted high
  To catch the alien's eye.   •

XIV.

The truant lad with dimpled cheek and chin,
And school-books satchel-cased, or elbowed in,
 And idle brain,
 You seek to stimulate in vain,
And schemes chaotic all innumerable
No tongue can tell;
 His text-books thrown aside,
 And threatened penalties defied,
  Lies basking in the sun,
  His task not done;

While tingling warm his lazy blood he feels,
From head to heels.
He gathers daisies in his hands,
And weaves them into chains and bands;
An idle tune he whistles,
Then snuffs the breath of new-blown thistles;
Or puffs the ripe ones on the air,
To scatter everywhere,
And leave their seeds
On farmers' meads.
He durst not seek the town,
Until the sun goes down.
Self-exiled he
Through larger liberty.
Some day, you leave him at a college-gate,
As though to his uncertain fate,
Youth's bloom upon his cheek,
His upper lip scarce brown
With manhood's down,
And back to business go;
The next, the lad you seek,
You'd scarcely know.
He stands a man,
Equipped your equal, stretch you how you can,
Is iron-muscled, where your arm is weak,
Erect on legs,
To try his muscle the spectator begs;
Has new ways of pronouncing Greek;
Can Darwin and can Huxley quote;
Is first-stroke of the College boat,
Thinks it is not good form to vote;
Can turn your logic inside out;
Like Hamlet he can spout,
Can strut the stage,
Soliloquize and rage,
As though he knew life's every page.
To trip him up, in vain you seek,
Though you on him your worn-out learning wreak.
For Art has done her perfect work in him,

Taught him each modern fashion, modern whim;
Informed his brain, and muscled every limb;
And filled him with life's wine up to the very
    brim.

xv.

Nature is but a foster-mother to the child,
    Who haunts her precincts fatherless;
    She cannot comfort his distress,
    The secret of it cannot guess.
        And when his heart she has beguiled
           With all the richness of her hoard,
Brought him the treasures of the seas,
His every sense to please;
Lapped him in luxury and ease;
    Brought oil to make his face to shine,
    And mantling wine,
    That he may dream himself divine;
        Taught him the poet's rhythmic phrase,
        The artist's imitative ways;
        And drugged him with her fulsome praise,
           His thirst she cannot slake,
           His heart still keeps its ache.
    Uncomforted,
    He lays his head
Within her lap, and sobbing cries
To think of past remembrances;
    Of aspirations fond
    His finite powers beyond;
    Of vanished gleams
From out his childhood dreams;
Of many a purpose crossed,
Of many a presence lost.
And though his brow she kiss
    With mother-fervor warm,
        And stroke his hair
        To ease discomfort there,
        His secret woe to share;

She has no magic charm or bliss,
Within the domains of her power
She has no dower;
She has no fascinating form
Of white-armed wife or supple child,
However fair and undefiled,
That can console
The yearning of his soul;
Make him heart-whole;
Make him forget
The echoes lingering in his bosom yet.

XVI.

Though Art and Nature strive in vain
To ease man's pain,
Before the night shall fold
The earth to rest
And set her stars as tapers at the head
Of some queen-sleeper dead,
The troubles of whose breast
Have met their last arrest,
Whose pulse of pride
Has fluttered out and died;
Before the sinking sun shall flush with red
The mountains cold,
As when a radiance faint
Passes across the face
Of some departing saint,
And leaves it touched to a celestial
grace,
'T is mortal's privilege to kneel again,
And tell to God life's struggles and life's pain;
To gird himself anew
For what he has on earth to do;
For what he has on earth to dare,
By humble prayer;
Before he sleep to be forgiven,
And shrived by the Great High-Priest for Heaven.

XVII.

The worlds that wheel in light,
Set in the deep-blue vistas of the night,
　　Are rounded by a law
　　Which knows no fleck or flaw:
　　　　The law that forms the pearl
　　　　　That's pendent in the ear
　　　　Of some proud daughter of an earl,
　　Who walks an orange-blossomed bride,
　　Her plighted lover by her side,
　　Proud with all her father's pride;
　　With all the pride of the ancestral tide
　　That stains
The purple of her veins;
　　Which quick responsive flushes
　　Her cheek with virgin blushes;
　　　　Sends hints of the unfolding rose
　　　　Across her temples' snows;
　　Or lights her kindling eyes
　　With oldtime chivalries:
The law that forms the drop
That quivers in the daisy's top;
　　That forms the tear,
That beads upon the face of some poor girl,
　　Distracted by unreal fear:
　　　　Some threat of mate
　　　　Ingrate,
　　Or frown of man severe: —
And God himself, had He no plan
In making man?
　　No purpose to fulfill
　　In human life and human will?
And when in that first image made,
Man is again arrayed,
　　And stands symmetrical,
　　The noblest of God's creatures all,
Is this some accident?

An arrow shot that overwent
The mark, or fell half-spent?

XVIII.

Some airy dome to spring,
    To shape Apollo by the chisel's stroke,
Cut out of marble rare
An Ariadne fair,
    To dare the poet's rhythmic flight
    Till lost to common sight,
And high majestic numbers sing;
    To pile up consecrated stone,
    To be o'erthrown
As some ephemeral thing
By shiver of the troubled planet which she momentary
    feels,
Majestic onward as she wheels;
        To gather heaps of pelf,
        Hide them in coffers, pile them on the shelf;
    Was it for this, God out of silence broke,
    Creation's final mandate spoke,
        And made the man in likeness to Himself?
    Climbed up Creation's stair,
    And left him crowned and princely there?

XIX.

In white effulgence almost hid,
    Excess of light
    Too clear for sight,
        There stand the Alps,
    Like hooded monks, who chant all night
        In monotone
        Hymns for the ear of God alone ·
        Lifting their snowy scalps
    The stars amid;
The stars which nightly rise and fall,
As though to weave their coronal.
        There stand the Alps; against their timbered feet,

Where wood and hamlet meet,
Man's surging life,
His insect toil and strife,
Breaking in little spray,
Then dying on the air away.
The glacier purple-pale,
Goes grinding to the vale;
On its unnoticed pilgrimage,
Descending to the very edge
Of sheltered chalet sweet;
Where'er its liberated waters flow,
Tingling the face of beauty to a glow,
Feeding the roots of vines and flowers
Through all the summer hours;
Cooling the brow that beads
Responsive to earth's daily needs;
Tossing the tiny ships
That childhood in its water dips;
And stealing to the lower vale
With benedictions that do never fail.
There stand the Alps; deep-rooted where
the earth
Had out of chaos its vulcanic birth;
Felt first primeval throes,
And into order rose.
There stand the Alps; when daylight comes
and goes
Empurpled in their lone repose;
As though God kissed their peaks anew,
When day first broke and when withdrew;
As earth's true fatherhood
Kisses home's little brood,
To show 't is reconciled
To ev'ry sev'ral wayward child;
The Alps, God's unpolluted shrines
Where on death's cold confines,
He sets his everlasting signs;
To touch man's soul to issues high,

And fit him for the sky.
Thus strong they, and immaculate,
They seem Heaven's solid gate,
The while his art goes crumbling to its fate.

XX.

Will come the fateful hour
When all the fabrics of man's puny power,
That build themselves in earth, or skyward tower,
His temples and cathedrals grand,
Far-sought from every land,
    His spires prolonged that pierce so high,
    His domes that simulate the sky
    Shall all in common ruin lie;
His statues topple down,
His pillars lose their ornamental crown,
His colonnades be overthrown,
    And his entablatures shall fractured be,
    As though in veriest mockery;
    Like childhood structures by the sea
        The swelling tides efface
        And leave no sign or trace.
        Become as his creations must,
        Like other dust;
    Go back again from sight and sense
    To the first elements;   '
        To Time's last tomb,
        In Nature's hungry womb;
    Himself alone
    Still to be known
Sole heir of immortality.
    Beyond the art of Rome or Greece,
    His Maker's masterpiece;
Greater than poet's thought;
Than Iliad and the Odyssee,
With swell like the Ægean sea;
Than Dante's love that lives in verse
    For all the ages to rehearse;

www.ingramcontent.com/pod-product-compliance
Lightning Source LLC
Chambersburg PA
CBHW022149090426
42742CB00010B/1445

Than Shakespeare's vast, dramatic throng,
Than Milton's sole, high-thoughted song;
Fairer than statue out of marble wrought,
Grander than grandest temple to perfection brought;
Than Carnak's fane or Parthenon,
Than life on canvas or than life in stone;
His aspirations satisfied
In Him who was and is and once on Calv'ry died!

XXI.

Than is St. Peter's dome,
The pride of Rome,
Fane forth from pagan fragments brought,
Greater the brain,
Which wrought
With throes of pain
That span's creative thought;
That swung its arches in the air,
And left them there,
As yet when they were not;
As flexible to sight,
As though of rays of palpitating light.
And God
Is greater than the skies He stretched abroad,
The seas He hollowed with his hands,
The islands and the continental lands;
Suggests Himself to finite eyes,
Then hides in His infinities.
Dwells He in man,
And not beneath St. Peter's span.
Of that celestial land of lands,
That house not made with hands
We read: No temple stands within,
No altar smokes for sin,
No chimes cathedral with their vibrant powers,
Pulsate the golden summer hours,
Where by Life's River stands the Tree,
Whose leaves drop balm,

Man's woes to soothe, his griefs to calm;
Whose ripest fruit is immortality.
The Lamb that once was slain,
Still signed with Calv'ry's sevenfold stain,
    He is the temple; and the pillars are
    Gathered from near and far,
        From all climes neath the sun
        In Him whose death makes all things one:
            The saints in light,
                Who 've washed their robes and made
                them white,
And breathe with Him that upper air,
Transfigured fair.
        And man,
        He is the culmination of God's plan,
        The prototype,
            When all things now are ripe:
At length, complete,
The Universe beneath his feet,
        Made one and whole,
        And mirrored in his soul;
The good, the beautiful, the true
    In Nature, Life, and Art,
    Fulfilling each its part,
Ever the same, yet ever new,
Running the whole Creation through:
        Breaking no more, as break discordant sees
        Their divers cadences,
But, by long patience tempered sweet,
    Eternal taught to rise,
    In sovereign harmonies,
        And blend in one
        Around the Great Creator's throne.